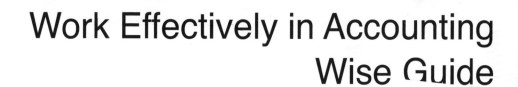

Work Effectively in Accounting
Wise Guide

AAT Level 2 Certificate i

Image of owl © Eric Isselée-Fotolia.com

Published by Osborne Books Limited, Unit 1B Everoak Estate, Bromyard Road, Worcester
Tel 01905 748071, Email books@osbornebooks.co.uk, Website www.osbornebooks.co.uk

Printed and bound by Mimeo, UK.

ISBN 978 1909173 002

how to use this Wise Guide

This Wise Guide has been designed to supplement your Tutorial and Workbook. It has two main aims:

■ to reinforce your learning as you study your course

■ to help you prepare for your online assessment

This Wise Guide is organised in the specific topic areas listed on pages 4 and 5. These individual topic areas have been designed to cover the main areas of study, concentrating on specific areas of difficulty. There is also an index at the back to help you find the areas you are studying or revising.

The Owl symbolises wisdom, and acts as your tutor, introducing and explaining topics. Please let us know if he is doing his job properly. If you have feedback on this material please email books@osbornebooks.co.uk

Thank you and good luck with your study and revision.

Osborne Books

●●●●●●●●●●●●●●●●●●●●●●●●●●●●●●●●●●

REVISION TIPS

'OWL' stands for: **O**bserve **W**rite **L**earn

There are a number of well-known ways in which you can remember information:

- *You can remember what it looks like on the page. Diagrams, lists, mind-maps, colour coding for different types of information, all help you **observe** and remember.*

- *You can remember what you **write** down. Flash cards, post-it notes around the bathroom mirror, notes on a mobile phone all help. It is the process of writing which fixes the information in the brain.*

- *You can **learn** by using this Wise Guide. Read through each topic carefully and then prepare your own written version on flash cards, post-it notes, wall charts – anything that you can see regularly.*

- *Lastly, give yourself **chill out** time, your brain a chance to recover and the information time to sink in. Promise yourself treats when you have finished studying – a drink, chocolate, a work out. Relax! And pass.*

list of contents

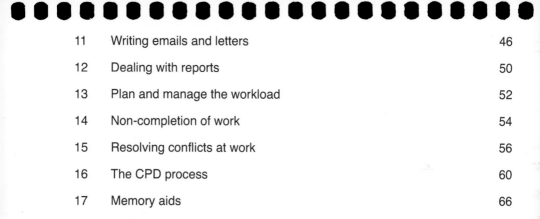

1   The accounting function

THE FUNCTIONS OF AN ACCOUNTING DEPARTMENT

*An Accounting Department carries out a number of important **functions** within an organisation – managing money and recording and reporting how money is spent. An Accounting Department also provides support to other parts of the organisation and information to external bodies such as banks and the tax authorities. These functions cover four main areas of activity . . .*

the four main areas of accounting activity

- **recording** financial data – writing up financial transactions in the accounts, eg sales and purchases

- **reporting** financial data – analysing financial data, eg sales figures, amounts outstanding from customers

- **forecasting** financial data – preparing budgets and forecasts of future performance

- **monitoring and control** – seeing if the forecasts are correct and taking action if they are off target

the main types of accountant

The accounting function deals with accounting information which relates to the past, the present and the future. Different types of accountant deal with this information in different ways.

FINANCIAL ACCOUNTANT

■ deals with **past** accounting data

■ prepares reports for **internal** managers and **external** bodies

MANAGEMENT ACCOUNTANT

■ deals with past and **future** accounting data

■ prepares budgets for managers and **internal** use

AUDITOR

■ checks that past and current accounting data and processes are correct

■ either **internal** or **external**

accounting functions and the information they provide

The diagram below sets out the accounting functions (areas of activity) that take place in an organisation. It also sets out the types of information these functions provide internally within an Accounting Department and also to other Departments in the organisation.

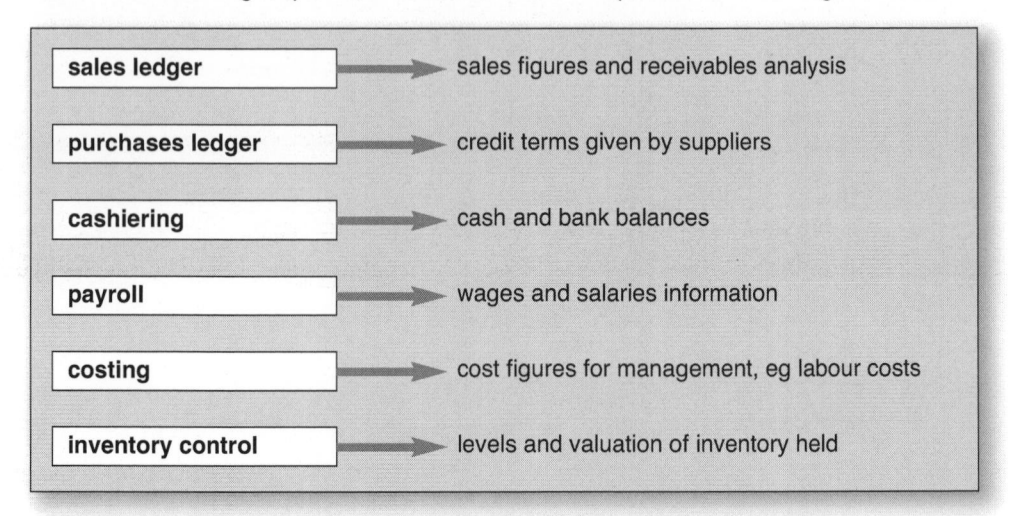

sales ledger	sales figures and receivables analysis
purchases ledger	credit terms given by suppliers
cashiering	cash and bank balances
payroll	wages and salaries information
costing	cost figures for management, eg labour costs
inventory control	levels and valuation of inventory held

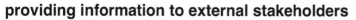

providing information to external stakeholders

A **stakeholder** is a person or body which has an interest in an organisation.

The Accounting Department of an organisation will also be responsible for providing financial and accounting information to a number of external 'stakeholders'.

The diagram below shows the type of information that is required.

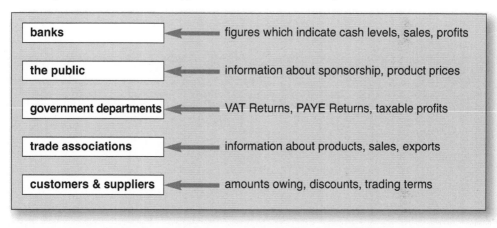

banks	←	figures which indicate cash levels, sales, profits
the public	←	information about sponsorship, product prices
government departments	←	VAT Returns, PAYE Returns, taxable profits
trade associations	←	information about products, sales, exports
customers & suppliers	←	amounts owing, discounts, trading terms

the importance of effective communication

Successful communication is **effective** communication – it achieves its aim by:

- being in the **appropriate format** (see pages 47 to 51 for examples of formats)
- being **clearly expressed** and easily understood
- giving the **correct message**
- being provided **at the right time** – not too early and not too late

This applies equally to:

- **internal** communications with colleagues, managers, other departments
- **external** communications – with customers, suppliers, banks

remember!

Effective communication means that information provided should be:

- *complete*
- *accurate*
- *on time*

AN EFFECTIVE ACCOUNTING DEPARTMENT

*An effective Accounting Department is one where all employees work as a team, treating each other with respect, knowing about and following all the **rules**, **procedures** and **legal requirements**. As a result mistakes will be kept to a minimum and the whole department will run smoothly.*

smooth running

An organisation that runs 'smoothly' means that there are few errors and disruptions to the normal flow of work.

Inevitably there will be unexpected events which will slow things down – fire alarms, computer breakdowns, illnesses, for example. A well-organised department will be able to cope with these problems by prioritising tasks.

Prioritising is dealt with in the Section 'Plan and manage the workload' (pages 52 to 53).

examples of smooth running

The diagram below shows areas of a typical Accounting Department which benefit from staff following **policies and procedures**, which are often set out in writing (see pages 14 - 15). These ensure smooth running by avoiding:

■ **errors** – which can occur if work is not checked for accuracy

■ **omissions** – which can occur if the work is not authorised, eg by a line manager

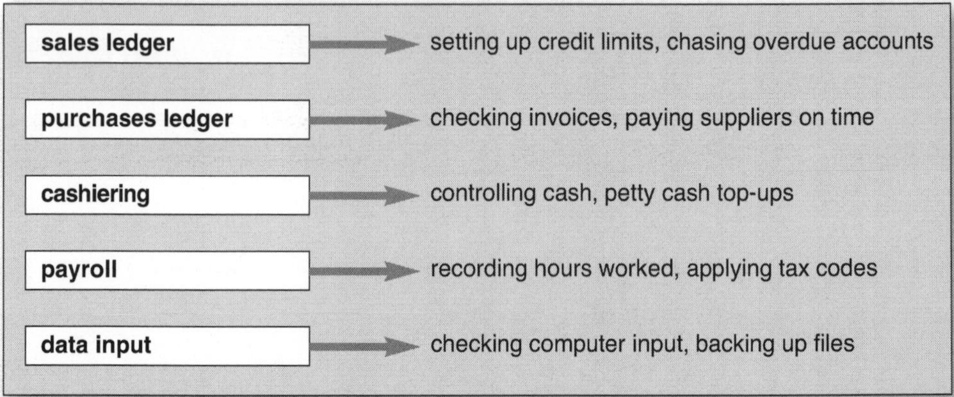

sales ledger	→ setting up credit limits, chasing overdue accounts
purchases ledger	→ checking invoices, paying suppliers on time
cashiering	→ controlling cash, petty cash top-ups
payroll	→ recording hours worked, applying tax codes
data input	→ checking computer input, backing up files

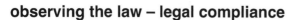

observing the law – legal compliance

Employees and employers of an organisation are also regulated by various areas of legislation. You do not need to know all the various individual laws but you do have to be aware of the areas they relate to and how they may affect the way in which people work. The most important of these areas of legislation are shown below.

Health & Safety at Work Act (HASAW)	This sets out the responsibilities of both employers and employees in the workplace. It covers areas such as safety in working areas and the reporting of accidents at work.
Data Protection Act	This regulates the way in which organisations deal with personal data relating to individuals. It requires strict **confidentiality**. It reinforces the principle of **confidentiality** which prevents the passing on of private information.
Working Time Regulations	These regulations set out the limits for working hours which employers and employees must observe. It covers areas such as maximum hours and the need for regular breaks.

3 Policies and procedures

KEEPING TO THE RULE BOOKS

*The Accounting Department, along with other departments in an organisation will normally be guided by 'rule book' documents known as **Policies and Procedures**. These are practical guides drawn up within the organisation which help it run smoothly and comply with legal requirements.*

types of Policies and Procedures

There are two main types of *Policies and Procedures* documents:

- Policies and Procedures that relate to **the Department** itself – for example an Accounting Department is likely to have Policies and Procedures setting out safeguards for cash handling and authorisation limits for making payments and cheque signing

- Policies and Procedures that relate to **the whole organisation** itself – for example, a Health & Safety manual, a Code of Conduct, a Sustainability Policy document

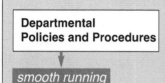

Departmental Policies and Procedures

smooth running

Policies and Procedures for the **Accounting Department**:

- authorisation limits for placing purchase orders
- authorisation limits for making bank payments
- writing and signing cheques
- dealing with cash

Organisational Policies and Procedures

smooth running

legal compliance

Policies and Procedures for the **organisation**:

- **Health & Safety** Policy Manual which covers safe working practices, accidents at work, fire regulations
- **Code of Conduct** which covers acceptable and unacceptable behaviour at work, eg use of company internet access for personal use, not getting drunk
- **Grievance Procedures** which set out how to complain about other people at work
- **Data Protection Procedures** which set out the need to keep company information and personal data confidential
- **Sustainability Policies** which set out the need to save power and recycle materials such as paper and plastic

4 The importance of solvency

KEEPING SOLVENT

*The Accounting Department plays an important part in managing the flows of money in and out of the organisation. This is critical in maintaining the **solvency** of a business organisation – in other words the ability of the business to pay its debts when they are due to be paid.*

being solvent and becoming insolvent – cash flow

Solvency is a 'life and death' matter for an organisation such as a business:

- a **solvent** business is a business **that can pay its debts when they are due** and can be trusted in a trading relationship and given credit terms

- an **insolvent** business is a business that cannot pay its debts and no other business will wish to trade with it. It is likely to be taken to an insolvency court:
  - if the business is an individual it could be made **bankrupt**
  - if it is a limited company it could go into **administration** or **liquidation**

- **cash flow** is money **flowing in** and **flowing out** of an organisation's bank account

- an Accounting Department must **control** the **timing** of money coming in and out of an organisation so that debts can be paid and the organisation remain **solvent**

- an Accounting Department will use a **cash flow forecast** which calculates the flows of money in and out of the organisation's bank account:

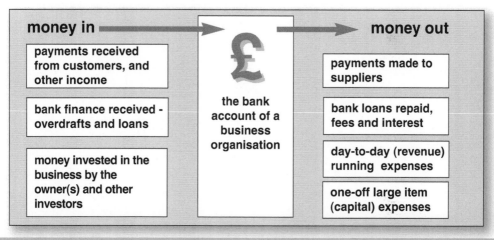

improving the cash flow

A successful Accounting Department will improve **cash flow** and **solvency** through

■ **timing** – making sure money received comes in as soon as possible

– making sure money is not paid out sooner than it needs to be

■ **efficiency** – reducing costs as much as possible

– maximising income as much as possible

The diagram on the next page shows:

■ Ways in which an **effective** Accounting Department can **improve** cash flow and an organisation's **solvency**.

These are the actions listed on the left.

■ Ways in which a **less effective** Accounting Department will **reduce** cash flow and make the organisation less **solvent**.

These are the actions listed on the right.

●●●●●●●●●●●●●●●●●●●●●●●●●●●●

improving cash flow = improving solvency	reducing cash flow = reducing solvency
encouraging credit customers to pay on time, or earlier (eg by giving settlement discounts)	not chasing up late payment of debts from credit customers, increasing customer discounts
negotiating longer credit terms (ie paying suppliers later)	paying suppliers earlier than is necessary
paying in money received into the bank as soon as possible	failing to pay money into the bank when it is received
minimising financial costs: - taking out low interest loans - avoiding fines for late VAT returns	incurring extra financial costs: - taking out high interest loans - receiving fines for late VAT Returns

5 Reporting lines

THE IMPORTANCE OF INFORMATION FLOWS

In any organisation it is important that information flows freely and promptly within the same department and also between different departments.

The information can pass on the same level, for example, between assistants, and also up and down the organisation between managers and assistants.

*These information links are known as **reporting lines**.*

types of information flow

Information is often a two-way process which can involve:

- ▪ instructions and requests within one department or to another department
- ▪ information provided and actions taken and confirmed
- ▪ instructions and requests within one department or to another department
- ▪ problems reported and sorted out within one department or with another department

lines of reporting within an organisation

There are two main directions that lines of reporting can take within an organisation:

- vertical reporting
- horizontal reporting

The example below shows how **vertical reporting** works in an Accounting Department.

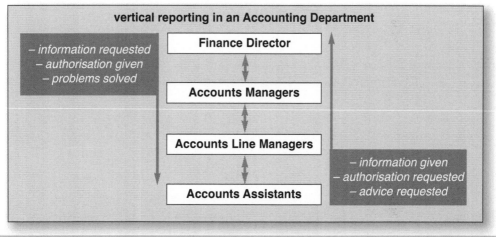

vertical reporting in an Accounting Department

- information requested
- authorisation given
- problems solved

Finance Director

Accounts Managers

Accounts Line Managers

Accounts Assistants

- information given
- authorisation requested
- advice requested

This diagram gives examples of how **horizontal reporting** works in an organisation.
Note how this can involve more than one department.

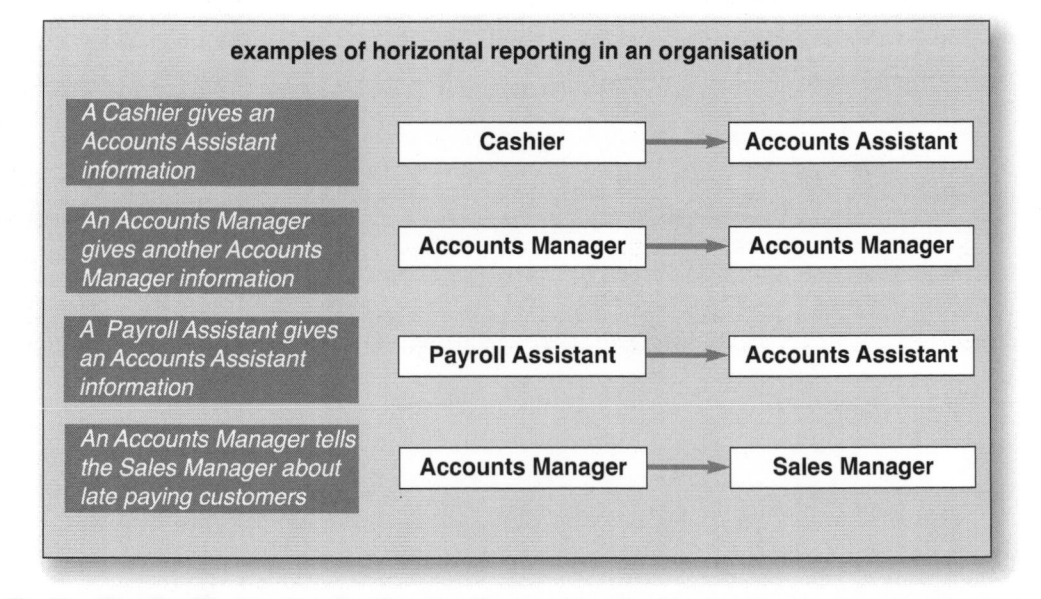

This diagram gives a couple of examples of how **horizontal and vertical reporting** can combine in the exchange of information between:

- two departments – Sales Department and Accounting Department
- two different levels of authority – Manager and Assistant

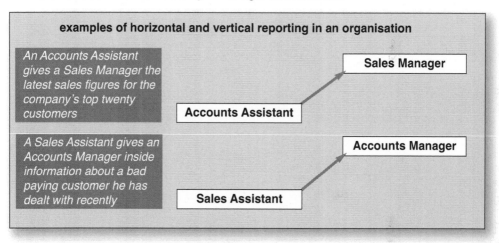

examples of horizontal and vertical reporting in an organisation

An Accounts Assistant gives a Sales Manager the latest sales figures for the company's top twenty customers

Sales Manager

Accounts Assistant

A Sales Assistant gives an Accounts Manager inside information about a bad paying customer he has dealt with recently

Accounts Manager

Sales Assistant

6 Working with numbers – the basics

WORKING WITH NUMBERS – AN ESSENTIAL SKILL

Working with numbers is an essential skill for anyone employed in an accounting or finance environment.

Working with numbers involves not only the basic arithmetic of addition, subtraction, multiplication and division, but also the ability to think in terms of proportions – calculating percentages and ratios.

arithmetic – basic operations

operation	symbol	example
addition	+	500 + 100 = 600
subtraction	−	500 − 100 = 400
multiplication	x	500 x 100 = 50,000
division	÷	500 ÷ 100 = 5

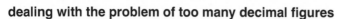

dealing with the problem of too many decimal figures

When carrying out calculations in accounting, you will often be dealing with money amounts, which involve a number with two decimal places (ie two numbers to the right of the decimal point) which represent pence or cents, for example £41.<u>42</u>.

But some calculations involving currency may produce figures with more than two decimal places, for example £12.<u>487</u>

The question is . . . how to reduce this amount to two decimal places?

the solution – the process of rounding

Rounding is reducing the number of decimal places of a number. All you need to do is:

■ decide the number of decimal places you need, eg two decimal places for pence; if the number has more than this number of decimal places, you should . . .

■ identify the last digit you want to keep, this is the 8 in the case of £12.4<u>8</u>7

■ leave it unchanged if the next digit is less than 5 (this is 'rounding down')

■ or, increase it by 1 if the next digit is 5 or more (this is 'rounding up')

■ in the above example of £12.<u>487</u>, as the third decimal place is 7 (and is higher than 5), it is rounded up by adding 1 to the 8 to produce £12.<u>49</u>

examples of rounding of figures to <u>two decimal places</u>

■ 20.549 rounded to two decimal places is 20.55

■ 20.543 rounded to two decimal places is 20.54

It is also possible to round numbers with decimal figures to **one decimal place**.

The same rounding rules apply, but in this case the second decimal figure is rounded up or down accordingly to produce a single decimal figure to the right of the decimal point.

The example below carries on using the figures in the example above, rounding the second decimal figure to a first decimal figure.

examples of rounding of figures to <u>one decimal place</u>

■ 20.55 rounded to one decimal place is 20.6

■ 20.54 rounded to one decimal place is 20.5

another method – rounding decimal figures to <u>the nearest whole number</u>

Most figures quoted are **whole numbers**, eg 4, 16, 256

A **whole number** is the number to the left of the decimal point. When rounding to the nearest whole number you do not round up or down the decimal figures from the **right** as on the previous page, but carry out the following procedure:

■ look at the figure to the **immediate right** of the decimal point, eg 10.<u>4</u>9

■ if that figure is less than 5, then the whole number remains the same; here it is 10

■ if the figure to the immediate <u>right</u> of the decimal point is 5 or more than 5, then the whole number is increased by 1

> **examples of calculating numbers to <u>the nearest whole number</u>**
>
> ■ 20.69 to the nearest whole number is 21
>
> ■ 20.59 to the nearest whole number is 21
>
> ■ 20.49 to the nearest whole number is 20

MEASURING PROPORTIONS

*Accounting often involves comparing proportions in the form of numbers –
for example 'How much profit did we make compared with sales?' or 'What
proportion of our employees are still paid in cash?' Rather than quoting
actual numbers it is often clearer if you convert the proportions to ratios,
fractions and percentages.*

- A **ratio** shows the proportional relationship between two figures; eg if four people
  have a meal and one has a nut allergy, the ratio of people with a nut allergy to
  those who do not is 'one to three' written as 1 : 3.

- A **fraction** shows the two numbers which are the part and the whole, eg if four
  people have a meal and one has a nut allergy, the fraction of people with the
  allergy is $\frac{1}{4}$; the top number is the part and the bottom number is the whole.

  Note that a fraction is different to a ratio – the **fraction** compares the **part and the
  whole** (the 1 and the 4) but a **ratio** compares the **two parts** (the 1 and the 3).

■ A **percentage** compares two numbers (a part and a whole) where the whole is expressed as 100. The phrase 'per cent' means 'out of every hundred'.

The formula used to calculate a percentage is:

$$\frac{\text{the part} \times 100}{\text{the whole}} \qquad = \qquad \text{percentage of the part}$$

Using the nut allergy example of one person in 4, the whole (4 people) becomes 100 and the part (one person) is calculated as 25%:

$$\frac{1 \times 100}{4} \qquad = \qquad 25\%$$

EXAMPLE

A business has 5 main customers; 4 of them pay up on time and 1 always pays late.

■ the **ratio** of late payers to customers who pay on time is 1 : 4

■ the **fraction** of late payers to total customers is $^1/_5$

■ the **percentage** of late payers is

$$\frac{1 \times 100}{5} \qquad = \qquad 20\%$$

working with percentages

Set out below are some common examples of the use of percentages in accounting.

■ working out a **percentage** of a **given number**, for example calculating discounts and VAT on invoices and credit notes

■ working out the **percentage** amount contained in an amount which has already had the percentage added on, for example working out the VAT charged for a purchase when only the total amount is shown on the receipt.

EXAMPLE: working out the VAT on an invoice

A business issues an invoice to a customer. The invoice total after the deduction of trade discount is £120. What is the VAT amount which is added to this total? (VAT is charged at 20%).

■ the **formula used is**:

$$\frac{\text{VAT percentage} \times \text{amount}}{100} = \text{percentage amount (ie the VAT)}$$

the calculation is: $\dfrac{20 \times £120}{100} = £24 \text{ VAT}$

EXAMPLE: working out the VAT content on a sales receipt

A business buys fuel at a service station and receives a receipt rather than the usual VAT invoice. The receipt does not show the VAT content but just a total of £84, which includes the VAT.

What is the VAT amount included in this £84 total? VAT is charged at 20%.

■ the **formula used is**:

$$\frac{\text{VAT percentage} \times \text{total amount (£)}}{100 + \text{VAT percentage}} = \text{VAT content (£)}$$

the calculation is: $\dfrac{20 \times £84}{100 + 20} = £14 \text{ VAT}$

■ an **alternative formula** to obtain the 20% VAT content of an amount involves multiplying the amount which includes the VAT by the fraction $^{1}/_{6}$, in this case:

$$£84 \times \frac{1}{6} = \text{VAT content of £14}$$

or, simply divide £84 by 6 = VAT content of £14

8 Calculating averages

WHAT IS AN AVERAGE?

An average is a number which is typical of a series of numbers and which can, if required, be used in calculations relating to that series of numbers. Accounting often involves the use of averages, for example inventory valued at 'average cost of purchase' is typical of the value of inventory held by a business at any one time during a given period.

Averages can be calculated in three main ways: mean, median and mode.

■ The **mean** is probably the most common type of average and is calculated as:

the total of all the figures added up, divided by the number of figures

■ The **median,** less commonly used, is

the value of the middle figure in a series of figures

■ The **mode,** also less commonly used, is

the value that occurs most commonly in a series of figures

EXAMPLE: working out averages
A business is reviewing its staffing levels and training requirements. There are nine members of staff in the Accounting Department. Their ages range from 17 to 36, and the ages are shown below. Note how the different averages produced differ.

17   17   17   21   21   24   28   35   36

- the average age using the **mean formula** (total of all ages divided by the number of employees) is:

$$17 + 17 + 17 + 21 + 21 + 24 + 28 + 35 + 36 = \frac{216 \text{ years}}{9 \text{ employees}} = 24 \text{ years}$$

- the average age using the **median formula** (the middle value in the series) is:

17   17   17   21   **21**   24   28   35   36 = 21 years

- the average age using the **mode formula** (the most common value in the series) is:

17   17   17   21   21   24   28   35   36 = 17 years

9 Interpreting charts

THE USE OF CHARTS

Accounting involves reporting financial informations such as sales, profits and costs. Charts, which can easily be produced from spreadsheets, are often used to illustrate results and trends in results in a visual and meaningful way. It is often said that 'a picture is worth a thousand words'.

You are not likely to be asked to produce a chart, but you will need to know how the different types of chart can be used and interpreted.

types of chart

The types of chart explained in this section are:

■ The **line graph** – used for presenting a trend over time, eg sales figures

■ The **bar chart** – also used for presenting a trend over time, eg profit figures

■ The **pie chart** – used for presenting a percentage break-down of a single result, eg the regional sales figures (north, south, east, west, midlands) of a UK business

line graph

The simplest form of graph is the **line graph**, as shown below.

A line graph shows the relationship between **two sets of data**, eg sales and years.

One set of data (eg years) is always **fixed** and runs along the bottom 'x axis'. The other (eg sales measured in money) will **vary** each year and is recorded on the 'y' vertical axis.

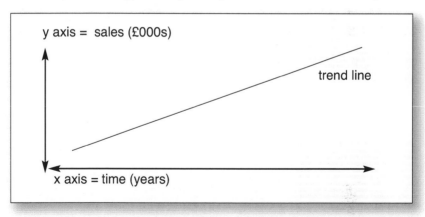

EXAMPLE

The following data has been provided:

Company Name   Amico Limited

Data given   Time period – Years 1, 2, 3 and 4 (horizontal 'x' axis)

Sales figures (vertical 'y' axis)	
	£000s
Year 1	500
Year 2	1,000
Year 3	1,400
Year 4	1,900

The line graph constructed from this data is shown on the next page.

Interpretation of the line graph

The sales have increased steadily from Year 1 to Year 2 from £500,000 to £1,900,000, as can be seen from the straight line which is inclined upwards.

EXAMPLE: line graph showing increasing yearly sales figures

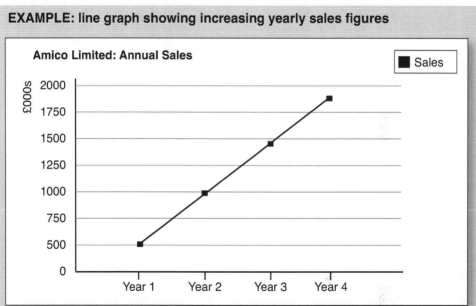

bar chart

A bar chart works on the same principle as a line graph, with fixed intervals on the horizontal axis and the variable data on the vertical axis, but instead of showing the trend as a line, the chart shows a series of bars.

The example below uses the same data as the line graph on page 37, and the chart clearly shows the same upward trend in sales.

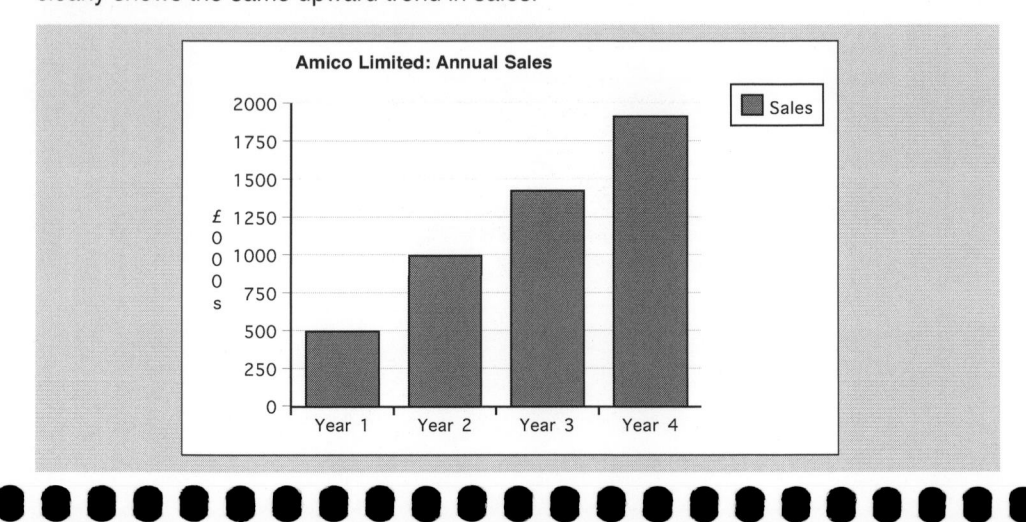

compound bar chart

Bar charts can be useful in showing trends for more than one variable at the same time. In the example below the sales figures for three different products, X, Y and Z, are shown over a four year period. It can be seen that Product Z does not sell so well, and in Year 4 the sales of Z have hardly increased at all, unlike the sales of the other products.

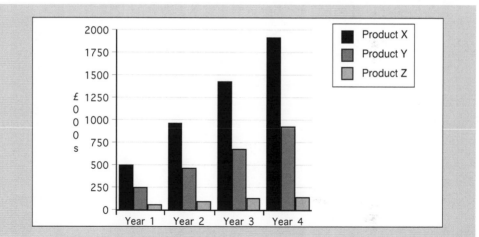

pie chart

A **pie chart** is a circle divided into sections to represent the parts of a whole in their correct proportions. It is called a pie chart because, like a pie, it is divided into 'slices'.

Pie charts are useful in showing the breakdown of a whole into a number of parts **at a particular moment in time**.

Pie charts differ from line graphs and bar charts, which present data which **varies** over a period of time and shows a **trend**. Pie charts cannot do this.

EXAMPLE

The Amico Limited divisional sales figures for Year 1 are as follows:

Division A	£300,000
Division B	£110,000
Division C	£90,000
Total sales	£500,000

The pie chart incorporating these figures is shown on the next page

pie chart notes

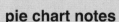

- the chart has labels showing the percentages rather than figures showing the actual results

- the chart shows very clearly the proportions of the sales made by the three divisions: Division A outsells the joint sales of the other two divisions

- there is no comparison of time periods – the chart only illustrates the breakdown of the Year 1 sales figures

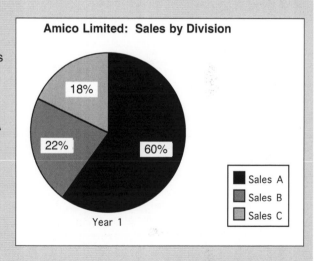

Amico Limited: Sales by Division

60%

22%

18%

Year 1

- Sales A
- Sales B
- Sales C

10 Using the language – basic rules

THE EFFECTIVE USE OF LANGUAGE

Working in accounting involves the use of written English in a number of ways – notes, emails, memos, letters and reports.

For the language to be effective it must be clear and accurate. The choice of words and style will vary with the type of communication used. It may be formal or informal, but it must be suitable for the situation and it must obey the basic rules of grammar.

basic rules – some problem areas

Problem areas include the use of the following words:

- its and it's

- there, they're and their

- too, to and two

its and it's

These two words are often confused:

- **its** is used to describe something that **belongs to** something else (it is like 'his' or 'her' but is used to apply to something that is not a person). For example:

    *'This dog is dangerous, **its** teeth are sharp and **its** bark is very loud.'*

    This means *'the teeth **of the dog** are sharp and the bark **of the dog** is very loud.'*

- **it's** is **a shortening** of 'it is' or 'it has'

    *'This dog is dangerous, **it's** jumping up at me and **it's** taken a bite out of my leg.'*

    This means *'**it is** jumping up at me and **it has** taken a bite out of my leg.'*

EXAMPLES

*'This assessment is hard, **it's** difficult to understand and **its** questions are too long.'*

*'The film I saw was terrible, **it's** too long, **it's** dull and **its** characters unconvincing.'*

*'This pasta is delicious, **its** flavour is great and **it's** not been overcooked.'*

---

there, they're and their

These three words are often confused:

- ■ **there** can be used with 'is' or 'are' – *'There is a cinema near here.'*
  there can also be used to describe where something is – *'It's over **there**.'*

- ■ **they're** is short for 'they are' – *'**They're** showing the latest Bond film.'*

- ■ **their** means 'belonging to them' – *'**Their** popcorn is to die for.'*

EXAMPLES

*'**There** is no business like show business.'*

*'**There** is the girl I was telling you about.'*

*'**They're** a hopeless team, always losing **their** matches.'*

*'**They're** eating **their** sandwiches over **there**.'*

*'**There** is no way **they're** going to share **their** sandwiches with us.'*

to, too, two

These three words are often confused:

- **to** can indicate direction – *'Walk **to** the end of the road with me.'*
  to can also be used as part of a verb – *'Thanks, I would like **to** walk with you.'*

- **too** can mean 'excessively' – *'You are walking far **too** quickly for me.'*
- **too** can mean 'as well' – *'But you are walking very quickly **too**!'*

- **two** is a number – *'**Two** is company, three is a crowd.'*

EXAMPLES

*'I know how **to** open a door while carrying **two** mugs of coffee.'*

*'I know how **to, too.**'*

*'**Too** many people have never learnt how **to** dance.'*

*'It takes **two to** tango.'*

---

11 Writing emails and letters

USING THE RIGHT LANGUAGE

Emails and letters are commonly used in an Accounting Department.

Both have set formats but letters are generally more formal in their use of language than emails. Both should use correct grammar and spelling.

You will need to be familiar with the format of both emails and letters and be able to judge the tone of the language to be used.

email language – what to avoid

When writing non-business emails the language used is very informal, often involving 'text-speak' and smileys. Business emails are far more formal and should **avoid**:

- **text language** – eg 'thks 4 yr email' – words should be spelt out in full
- **smileys :(**
- **OVERUSE OF CAPITAL LETTERS** – this, is called SHOUTING and looks ugly
- **too many exclamation marks !!!!!!!!!!!!!!!** – this is distracting and unnecessary

elements of an email

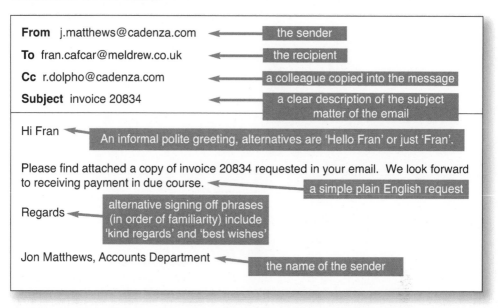

From j.matthews@cadenza.com ← the sender

To fran.cafcar@meldrew.co.uk ← the recipient

Cc r.dolpho@cadenza.com ← a colleague copied into the message

Subject invoice 20834 ← a clear description of the subject matter of the email

Hi Fran ← An informal polite greeting, alternatives are 'Hello Fran' or just 'Fran'.

Please find attached a copy of invoice 20834 requested in your email. We look forward to receiving payment in due course. ← a simple plain English request

Regards ← alternative signing off phrases (in order of familiarity) include 'kind regards' and 'best wishes'

Jon Matthews, Accounts Department ← the name of the sender

the business letter

Business letters are a very traditional form of communication and tend to be more formal than emails in their layout and language – see next page. They should include:

■ the **address** of the **sender** (normally printed at the top) and the **recipient**

■ the **date,** the **reference** (if there is one) of the sender and a **subject heading**

■ a **structured** message – opening paragraph, details of the letter, closing paragraph

■ a **salutation** ('Dear...') and **complimentary close** (yours sincerely, yours faithfully)

remember!

■ *salutation – this is the 'Dear Mr Cameron' or 'Dear Sir' line of the letter which addresses the person receiving it*

■ *complimentary close – this is the 'yours sincerely' or 'yours faithfully' part of the letter which signs it off; it fulfils the same function as the 'regards' line on an email*

■ *the rule for which complimentary close to use*

– *'Dear Mr Cameron' . . . 'Yours sincerely'*

– *'Dear Sir' or 'Dear Madam' . . . 'Yours faithfully'*

basic elements of a letter

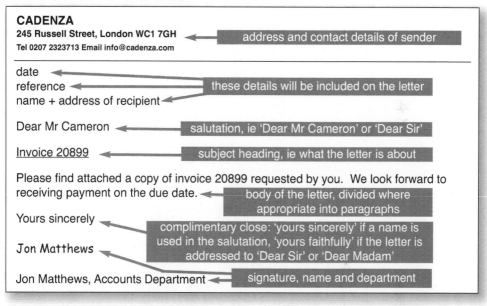

CADENZA
245 Russell Street, London WC1 7GH ← address and contact details of sender
Tel 0207 2323713 Email info@cadenza.com

date ←
reference ← these details will be included on the letter
name + address of recipient ←

Dear Mr Cameron ← salutation, ie 'Dear Mr Cameron' or 'Dear Sir'

Invoice 20899 ← subject heading, ie what the letter is about

Please find attached a copy of invoice 20899 requested by you. We look forward to receiving payment on the due date. ← body of the letter, divided where appropriate into paragraphs

Yours sincerely ← complimentary close: 'yours sincerely' if a name is used in the salutation, 'yours faithfully' if the letter is addressed to 'Dear Sir' or 'Dear Madam'

Jon Matthews ←

Jon Matthews, Accounts Department ← signature, name and department

THE USE OF REPORTS

Reports are produced from time-to-time in an Accounting Department. They may be one-off reports, eg 'Should we have a fully computerised accounting system?' or they may be regular short reports, eg for sales data. If you are working in an accounting environment you may not be required to write full reports, but you will be expected to know your way around a report and be able to interpret it and any charts included in it.

the sections of a report

▨ A **formal report** has **seven main sections**: Title page, Summary (or Executive Summary), Introduction, Findings, Conclusions, Recommendations and Appendices.

▨ A **less formal** report (eg a monthly sales report) may not have all of these sections.

▨ You will need to be familiar with the contents of **all seven sections** of a formal report. They can be confusing, because some of the section descriptions sound similar.

You should memorise the section contents on the next page.

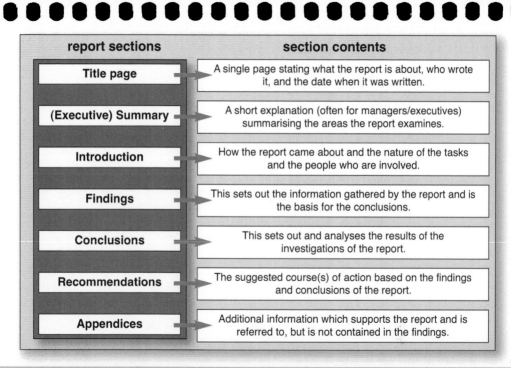

report sections	section contents
Title page	A single page stating what the report is about, who wrote it, and the date when it was written.
(Executive) Summary	A short explanation (often for managers/executives) summarising the areas the report examines.
Introduction	How the report came about and the nature of the tasks and the people who are involved.
Findings	This sets out the information gathered by the report and is the basis for the conclusions.
Conclusions	This sets out and analyses the results of the investigations of the report.
Recommendations	The suggested course(s) of action based on the findings and conclusions of the report.
Appendices	Additional information which supports the report and is referred to, but is not contained in the findings.

13 Plan and manage the workload

THE NEED TO PLAN

Working in any organisation means that you need to be organised. You will need to know what you have to do and when you have to do it. This is particularly true in an Accounting Department when so many processes are interdependent.

No day is the same, and so you will often need to prioritise tasks, causing minimum disruption to the office workflow and your colleagues.

types of task

There are a number of different types of task: some can be delayed if there is an unexpected problem, some cannot. Planning and prioritising involves being able to distinguish between these types:

- **routine** and **scheduled** tasks, eg processing invoices, can more easily be delayed
- **'one-off'** tasks, eg unblocking a toilet, normally take priority over routine tasks
- **urgent** tasks, eg providing figures for a manager for a meeting the same day, must always take priority

planning aids

It is impossible to plan efficiently if you just carry everything around in your head. There are many **planning aids** which enable employees and management to schedule tasks, both on a daily basis and also over the longer term. Each type of planning aid is best suited to a particular need. The diagram below sets out the most common planning aids.

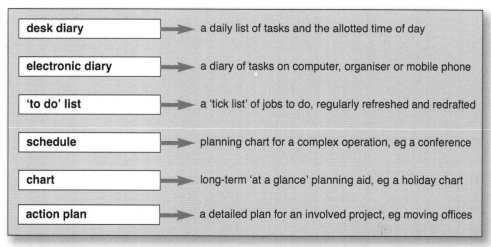

desk diary	a daily list of tasks and the allotted time of day
electronic diary	a diary of tasks on computer, organiser or mobile phone
'to do' list	a 'tick list' of jobs to do, regularly refreshed and redrafted
schedule	planning chart for a complex operation, eg a conference
chart	long-term 'at a glance' planning aid, eg a holiday chart
action plan	a detailed plan for an involved project, eg moving offices

14 Non-completion of work

THE NEED TO COMPLETE WORK

Working in an organisation means teamwork. If any member of the 'team' does not perform well, or at all, the consequences can be serious.

All employees need to realise that they have a responsibility to their colleagues – and to the organisation as whole – to complete their work, on time, and make a good job of it.

the impact of the completion of work tasks

An employee who completes the tasks that are set, on time, and to the required standard will bring benefits both to the employee and also to the organisation:

- the **employee** will feel personally satisfied and motivated
- **colleagues** will also benefit, not only from the 'feel good' factor, but also because they will not be held up in their own work, or have to correct mistakes
- **the organisation** will benefit from the productivity achieved

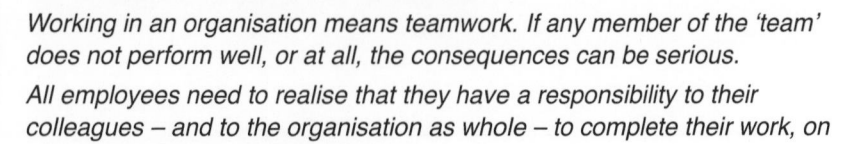

the impact of the non-completion of work tasks

An employee who fails to complete tasks that are set, on time, and to the required standard will cause a number of problems. Take, for example, an employee who makes mistakes when processing sales invoices on the computer . . .

■ the **employee** is likely to feel demotivated when he or she is criticised for poor work

■ the **employee** may fall out with colleagues because of the poor work

■ **colleagues** are likely to encounter problems themselves because the mistakes may:

– delay the production of invoices

– require them to process the invoices themselves if work has been held up

■ the **Accounting Department** will get a reputation for mistakes which will in turn demotivate the accounting staff

■ the **organisation** will incur costs for the extra time spent sorting out the mistakes and general loss of productivity

■ the **organisation** may lose sales if the mistakes go undetected – wrong goods may be sent out (incorrect inventory coding), or the wrong price may be charged

15 Resolving conflicts at work

CONFLICTS

Team-working in an organisation inevitably results in some form of conflict. This can be caused by a clash of personalities or a difference in methods of working.

Conflicts inevitably result in problems for the team, including non-completion of work and a fall in efficiency and performance.

Conflicts need to be resolved, either by team members themselves or by referral to a higher authority such as a Line Manager:

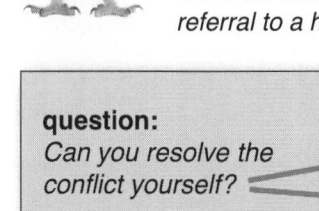

question:
Can you resolve the conflict yourself?

YES → sort out the problem with the person causing the problem

NO → refer the problem to the appropriate higher authority

causes of conflicts with colleagues and the organisation

There are many situations caused by colleagues which can potentially result in a conflict. For example a colleague may . . .

- fail to complete work on time
- make mistakes in his or her work
- ignore set procedures for carrying out tasks
- be critical of your work
- be anti-social, eg not wash up a coffee cup or have unpleasant personal habits
- be dishonest, eg steal from the petty cash tin
- be dishonest, eg steal your crisps
- be a bully or a sexist

In addition your quarrel may be with the **organisation** itself, for example:

- unfair treatment by the management
- being passed over for promotion on racial or sexist grounds

knowing whom to go to with your problem

All of the situations listed above are likely to cause problems for you and your other colleagues.

The question is knowing **whom to go to** (if anyone) in order to resolve the conflict.

The solutions are not clear-cut, and are likely to vary from organisation to organisation.

The following guidelines are suggested to help you with assessment questions.

personal questions to ask	possible solutions
Can I sort out this problem myself?	■ if you can, talk to the person and work out a solution
What if I cannot sort it out myself?	■ talk to colleagues about it ■ refer the matter to a Line Manager
Is the conflict caused by the Line Manager?	■ refer the matter to a more senior manager
Is the problem caused by the organisation itself?	■ consider taking the matter through the Grievance Procedure

EXAMPLE – conflict problems and possible solutions

Problems you can sort out yourself with your colleague →
- he works with an iPod turned up to a very high volume which you can hear
- you see her taking your cheese straws from the office fridge

Problems to refer to a Line Manager →
- your colleague constantly makes racist remarks
- you see your colleague regularly stealing money from petty cash

Problems to refer to a higher authority than a Line Manager →
- you consider that you are being bullied by your Line Manager
- you consider you are being unfairly treated at your appraisal

16 The CPD process

CONTINUING PROFESSIONAL DEVELOPMENT (CPD)

*Continuing Professional Development (CPD) is the **process** that employees undertake to **maintain and improve the knowledge and skills that they need in their professional work**.*

*The process is a **partnership** between the employer and the employee which should improve employee performance and benefit the employer.*

*It should be **discussed regularly** by the employee and employer.*

the four stages of CPD – an ongoing cycle

- identifying **development needs** – discussing weaknesses and areas to develop

- setting **objectives** – deciding on a development plan for a set period of time

- making the most of available **resources** – 'on-the-job' training, external training

- **reviewing progress** after a period of time – seeing how you have got on

These four stages are an **ongoing process**, often planned at an annual appraisal.

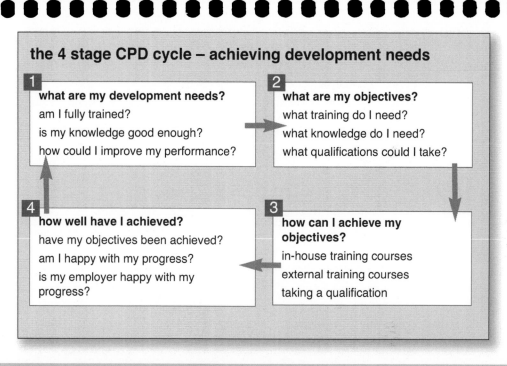

the 4 stage CPD cycle – achieving development needs

1

what are my development needs?

am I fully trained?

is my knowledge good enough?

how could I improve my performance?

2

what are my objectives?

what training do I need?

what knowledge do I need?

what qualifications could I take?

4

how well have I achieved?

have my objectives been achieved?

am I happy with my progress?

is my employer happy with my progress?

3

how can I achieve my objectives?

in-house training courses

external training courses

taking a qualification

Stage 1: discussing development needs

■ The first step is to discuss your skills and knowledge with your employer and establish your development needs.

■ Part of this process is to define your **strengths** and your **weaknesses**.

■ It is a good idea to write down your strengths and weaknesses, for example:

STRENGTHS	WEAKNESSES
working with figures	writing emails
working with colleagues	not confident dealing with customers on the phone
using spreadsheets	handling Word documents
organising socials	no professional qualifications

■ These strengths and weaknesses can then be used as a basis for discussion with the employer and the **setting of objectives**.

Stage 2: setting of CPD objectives

■ **Objectives** will be set by the employee in discussion with the employer

■ Objectives should be **SMART**:

    S   **Specific** – they should be clear and well-defined so that they can be monitored and the employee's success measured.

    M   **Measurable** – the employee and the manager should be able to tell how well the objective is being achieved as time goes on.

    A   **Achievable** – the objective must be realistic and the resources must be provided by the management (eg time, access to people, course fees).

    R   **Realistic** – can the employee realistically cope with the objectives that have been set?

    T   **Timely** – can the objective be achieved within the time target?

■ Objectives should be formally **recorded** by the employer so that they can be monitored as time passes and progress (or lack of it!) noted.

Stage 3: resources for skills and knowledge development

There are a wide range of resources available which enable employees to meet their CPD objectives. These can be:

■ time-based resources: time is a costly resource provided by employer and employee

■ physical resources: computer access, books and other learning materials

It will be the task of the employer and employee together to plan out and obtain the necessary resources.

employer resources

■ on-the-job training (sitting with a colleague)

■ in-house formal training courses

■ funding of external formal training courses and qualifications

employee resources

■ personal reading and research – online or from books

■ evening classes, studying for a qualification

■ distance learning courses

Stage 4: monitoring achievement – and further planning

The last stage in the CPD cycle is to check periodically that the objectives set have been, or are being, achieved. This can be done in a number of ways, normally through the Line Manager:

- **informal feedback**
  - from the employee at any time during the year, eg problems with a training course (negative feedback), college award for student achievement (positive feedback)
  - comments from colleagues working in the same part of the organisation
  - feedback from other managerial staff who have contact with the employee

- **formal feedback**
  - formal annual appraisal session with the Line Manager
  - assessing performance against given criteria, eg achieving passes in professional exams and consequently receiving funding for the course fees

forward planning

The annual appraisal of the employee is not only a review of the year's progress, it is also the starting point for the CPD planning for the following year. The cycle starts again.

17 Memory aids

KEEPING YOUR MEMORY FIT

The human brain is an odd organ – you can remember the most useless facts, but when it comes to complex matters such as accounting procedures the mind can go completely blank. But it is possible to train your brain.

At the beginning of this Guide there are some revision tips which suggest that you can study effectively and recall information by . . .

■ ***Observing***, *ie remembering what information looks like on the page, using diagrams, lists, mind-maps and colour coding. Memory is very visual.*

■ ***Writing*** *information down, using flash cards, post-it notes, notes on a phone. It is the actual process of writing which helps to fix the information in the brain.*

■ ***Learning*** *by regularly going through your course notes and text books. Find a 'study buddy' in your class (or online) to teach and test each other as the course progresses.*

■ **Chill out** when you get tired. Give your brain a chance to recover. Get some exercise and fresh air, work out. In the ancient world there was the saying that "a fit body is home to a fit mind."

■ **Treats** – promise yourself rewards when you have finished studying – meet friends, eat chocolate, have a drink, listen to music.

exam preparation

■ **Practice, practice, practice** when preparing for your assessment.

Practice the questions and assessments in the Osborne Books workbooks.

Practice the free online assessments on the Osborne Books website:

Log on to www.osbornebooks.co.uk/elearning or scan this . . .

some aids to memory

On the next few pages are blank spaces for you to set out some of the important formulas, words and phrases you will need to memorise for your assessment.

1 FACTORS WHICH MAY AFFECT THE RUNNING OF AN ORGANISATION

Policies and procedures which an organisation may adopt	*Areas of law (eg statutes) which may affect the running of an organisation*

2 ACTIONS WHICH AFFECT THE SOLVENCY OF AN ORGANISATION

Actions which will IMPROVE the solvency of an organisation	Actions which will REDUCE the solvency of an organisation

3 FORMULAS FOR PERCENTAGES, AND AN EXAMPLE USING A 20% RATE

Formula for working out a percentage of a money amount	*Formula for working out a percentage amount contained in a total amount which has had the percentage added on*
worked example (using a 20% rate)	*worked example (using a 20% rate)*

4 FORMULAS FOR PERCENTAGES, AND AN EXAMPLE USING A 10% RATE

Formula for working out a percentage of a money amount	*Formula for working out a percentage amount contained in a total amount which has had the percentage added on*
worked example (using a 10% rate)	*worked example (using a 10% rate)*

72

4 THE SECTIONS OF A WRITTEN REPORT

Complete the boxes with the names of the sections of a report, in the correct order.

index